Original title:
Squirrel Scribbles

Copyright © 2025 Creative Arts Management OÜ
All rights reserved.

Author: Julian Prescott
ISBN HARDBACK: 978-1-80567-183-1
ISBN PAPERBACK: 978-1-80567-482-5

Notes from the Canopy

Swinging high in leafy light,
Nuts are stolen, never right.
Twisting tails and chatter loud,
Sassy spirits, daring proud.

Branches sway with silly dance,
Every leap, a daring chance.
Chasing shadows, wild and free,
Nature's jesters, you and me.

Whirlwinds in the Woods

Round and round the branches go,
Tiny acorns steal the show.
Spinning quick, a comic chase,
Hearts are racing, smiles on face.

Rustling leaves, a playful tease,
Tickling trunks, oh what a breeze.
Running here, then running there,
Laughter echoes through the air.

Scribbles Under the Sky

Doodles scrawled on nature's page,
Jumps and flips, they act their age.
Wiggly words on boughs so wide,
Adventures burst, they cannot hide.

Puffy clouds and giggles blend,
Witty tales that never end.
Nuts and dreams in lofty flight,
Jolly squirrely delight.

Chaotic Chasing

Through the trees, they dart and dash,
Little paws make quite a splash.
With a squeak and dash away,
Mischief brews, come join the play.

Chasing tails and sprightly leaps,
In the twilight, laughter creeps.
Join the fun, no time to rest,
In this caper, we are blessed.

Acorn Anthology

In the park where critters play,
Acorns tumble all the day.
Chasing one, I trip and fall,
Bouncing here, I've made a haul!

Tiny paws, so quick and spry,
In the chase, we zoom, we fly!
With a laugh, I tip my hat,
To the nut that squeaked, 'I'm flat!'

The Leafy Tapestry

Leaves are bigger than my head,
Wobbling as I seek my bed.
Tangled branches make me grin,
Lost in green, and still I spin!

A dance with wind, I lift and sway,
Swinging high, I shout hooray!
Through the foliage, laughter flows,
As I tumble, watch me go!

Patchwork of Paws

Paw prints scatter on the ground,
In this maze of leaves, I'm bound.
Over here and then we dart,
Guess my plan? I'll steal your heart!

Chasing shadows, quick as light,
Doing flips, oh what a sight!
Patchwork fur, and cheeky grins,
Among the nuts, let fun begin!

Tales from the Treehouse

Up the trunk, oh what a climb,
Gathering tales like bells that chime.
Secret meetings, bold and brash,
Sipping sunshine, feeling flash!

From my perch, I spy below,
Friends and foes, in quiet flow.
With a wink, I spin a tale,
In the treehouse, friendships sail!

The Romping Rascals

In the trees they leap and dash,
With acorn hats that flash and crash.
Tiny thieves with nimble grace,
Chasing shadows, what a race!

They chatter loud, they tease and play,
Making mischief every day.
With furry tails that twist and twirl,
Spinning round in a wild whirl!

Life's a game of hide and seek,
With playful antics all week.
They gather goodies, make a stash,
In their world, there's always a splash!

In the park, they roam with glee,
Crafty little characters, you see.
With a hop and skip, they wave goodbye,
Leaving laughter as they fly by!

The Stash of Secrets

In the hollow of an oak so grand,
Lies a treasure well hidden, a secret band.
Nuts and acorns from the forest floor,
Tiny troves collected and stored galore.

With a cheeky grin and a twitchy tail,
It races back home through valley and vale.
Guarding its trove from curious eyes,
In a world full of wonders, oh how it tries!

Nature's Notable Nibbler

Fluffy cheeks puffed like a furry balloon,
Chasing shadows beneath the bright moon.
Nibbling on snacks like a gourmet feast,
Who knew a critter could be such a beast?

With a hop and a skip, it scampers around,
In the great outdoors, it leaps off the ground.
Each tiny bite is a moment of fun,
Playing hide and seek 'til the day is done.

Flights of Fancy

Dancing on branches with effortless grace,
Wings of imagination, oh what a race!
Bounding and leaping from treetop to leaf,
Creating mischief, a joyful belief.

Catch me if you can, I'm fast as a flash,
Racing the sunlight through each little dash.
In whimsical worlds where laughter feels free,
You can't help but smile at the antics of me!

Portraits of Paws

Tiny paws paint pictures on forest trails,
Each wiggle and scamper tells curious tales.
A flash of a tail, a dash through the grass,
A masterful artist, my moments surpass.

With twirls and spins, I'm a sight to behold,
In the gallery of life, all stories unfold.
Framing the laughter in each little loop,
My joyful exploits, a delightful troop!

Sketches of the Savvy Forager

In a dance of blurry tails,
Nutty dreams fill tiny trails.
With a leap they chase the breeze,
Collecting snacks with perfect ease.

Cheeks stuffed full, they hide away,
Countless treasures in display.
A crafty nibble, a playful tease,
Master of finds, never to freeze.

Whimsical Whiskers

Upside down, they hang with glee,
Tickled by a friendly tree.
Fuzzy tails wave in the air,
Chasing shadows everywhere.

Bouncing high from branch to branch,
In their antics, none a chance.
Whiskers twitch in silly sights,
Creating joy in playful flights.

Laughter Among the Leaves

Rustling leaves hear them giggle,
As tiny paws take a wiggle.
Cartwheeling through nature's cheer,
They spread joy with every cheer.

Gathered nuts become a game,
In this frenzy, none feel shame.
With a hop, skip, and a grin,
Funny pints of joy begin.

The Eclectic Explorer

With a map made of pure twigs,
They set forth on daring jigs.
Peeking at the world around,
Adventures waiting to be found.

Every nook a brand new quest,
In their hearts, they feel so blessed.
From the garden to the park,
Many stories leave their mark.

Patterns in the Pine

In the trees, they twist and dive,
Little acrobats, so alive.
Chasing tails and hopping high,
With cheeky grins, they soar the sky.

Their tiny paws make quite the sound,
As they flick and flit all around.
Nutty stashes tucked away tight,
Planning their next comedic flight.

Tales of the Tiny Tread

Underneath the moon's soft glow,
Tiny paws make a charming show.
A misstep here, a jump to there,
Giggles trail in the crisp night air.

With every hop, a dance unfolds,
Their little antics, a joy retold.
In the garden, they find their games,
Creating laughter with silly names.

A Clamor of Creatures

In the morning light, they gather near,
Chirping secrets for all to hear.
With puffy cheeks and little leaps,
They share their tales while the world sleeps.

Through rustling leaves and fleeting glances,
They frolic in playful, silly dances.
A riot of chatter fills the air,
As they plot their next prank with flair.

The Leafy Notes of Nature

Among the trees, their chatter rings,
Whispers of mischief, oh, what fun brings!
Cracking jokes with every leap,
Their vibrant antics, a joy to keep.

With every rustle, they giggle and play,
In their leafy world, they frolic all day.
A symphony of squeaks fills the breeze,
Nature's jesters, at ease in the trees.

Fluttering Forepaws

In the tree, a tiny dance,
With a leap, a quick romance.
Chasing acorns, what a sight,
Fluffy tails in morning light.

They flick and flip, a bounding spree,
Oh, the joy of being free!
Branches sway beneath their play,
Chirping songs of bright array.

Adventures in Bark

A wooden plane, a daring climb,
Voyaging through the woods, sublime.
With bark as maps, they navigate,
Each twist and turn, they celebrate.

They spy a nut, a treasure gleam,
In their eyes, an urgent dream.
The race begins, oh what a rush,
To grab that prize in leafy hush.

The Folly of Forest Fragments

Bits of leaves and twigs askew,
In chaos, they all go 'Who knew?'.
One hops over, another near,
'Look at this mess!'—laughter, cheer.

A twig adorns a furry head,
Fashion statement, daily spread!
They strut around, with gleeful pride,
Nature's jesters, side by side.

Diary of a Diplomatic Rodent

Thank you cards from trees so tall,
Apologies for seeds that fall.
A peace treaty with the birds,
'No more ransacking of your herds!'

With tiny paws, they shake on it,
Laughing at their own little wit.
In forest halls, a giggle here,
These rodents charm both far and near.

Echoes of the Forest Floor

In the hush of the trees, critters play,
Jumping and tumbling, brightening the day.
With acorn hats and tails that dance,
Under a sunbeam, they prance and prance.

Leaves crackle softly, a stage for their jest,
A comedic display, nature's own fest.
Chasing each other, they leap with a cheer,
Whispers of laughter, can you hear them near?

Bindings of Twigs and Dreams

Nestled in canopies, dreams take their flight,
With twigs as their anchors, they float out of sight.
Tiny adventures, in the branches they weave,
Each knot tells a tale, oh what they believe!

Their giggles abound, as they scurry around,
In a world made of wonders, where merriment's found.
A festival of chuckles beneath leafy wraps,
With every small stumble, the whole forest claps!

The Capers of Cunning Creatures

Watch the acrobat dart in a flash,
Dancing through branches, making a splash.
With cheeks full of treasures, mischief in tow,
They giggle and wiggle, putting on quite a show.

Their tiny paws hustle, always in motion,
Crafting their antics, a joyous devotion.
Through nuts and the fluff from the big willow tree,
They concoct their plans like it's all meant to be.

Scribbles in the Sky

Above in the blue, they trace silly lines,
With imaginary chalk, making bold signs.
Clouds like canvas, a playground afloat,
Creating their stories, each whimsical note.

They leap for the stars, twirling with glee,
Drawing up laughter for all to see.
With a flick of their tails, they twirl and they spin,
In the laughter of skies, let the fun begin!

Echoes from the Elm

In the branches high they play,
Chasing shadows every day,
With acorn hats and bows of twine,
Their chatter's sweet, a silly rhyme.

They tumble down, a clumsy dance,
In leafy beds, they take their chance,
A nutty joke or two they'll tell,
In the old elm, they laugh so well.

With tiny paws, they scurry quick,
And tease the dog, it's quite the trick,
A pitter-patter, funny sound,
In every nook, more laughs abound.

When dusk arrives, they take their rest,
In cozy nests, so warmly blessed,
With dreams of nuts and playful schemes,
The elm stands tall, and all's a dream.

Tiny Footprints in the Dust

A hop, a skip, a tiny trace,
Like little dancers in a race,
They prance about from tree to tree,
With dust clouds whirling, wild and free.

Their tiny footprints mark the ground,
A little story, all around,
With trails of laughter and delight,
In every nook, they spark the night.

A curious glance, a playful stare,
They sneak around without a care,
With playful puffs, they scatter near,
Drawing smiles, spreading cheer.

As sunbeams dance on leaves so bright,
They poke their heads to greet the light,
In dust they frolic, spin, and twirl,
Tiny footprints in a giggle whirl.

The Tall Tale of Twigs

A tale to tell of twigs so tall,
That wink and dance at every call,
With chips and chews, they boast their skills,
Of forest feats and nutty thrills.

With every crack, a story spins,
Of daring leaps and cheeky grins,
They gather 'round and raise a cheer,
These twiggy tales we love to hear.

Around the bend, the mischief grows,
Of silly pranks and clumsy toes,
The tallest of twigs just might proclaim,
"I caught a breeze, I'm quite the game!"

With wild antics, laughter flies,
In every branch, a new surprise,
So gather 'round for tales of fun,
Of twigs and tricks, we'll never run.

Breezy Confessions

In breezy whispers, secrets shared,
Of nutty snacks and how they dared,
They laugh as leaves begin to sway,
With every gust, a funny play.

A chipmunk peeks, his eyes so wide,
As they're confessing side by side,
"I stole a treat, or was it two?"
The laughter bubbles, bright and true.

With every breeze, a tale's unfurled,
Of funny antics in their world,
A dance of joy beneath the sky,
Their breezy secrets soar and fly.

So let the whispers fill the air,
Of every nut and silly dare,
In breezy confessions, hearts rejoice,
As laughter echoes, a merry voice.

Leafy Postcards

In the breeze they float in grace,
A dance of green, they find their place.
Whispers of stories wrapped in curls,
Nature's letters, spun from twirls.

Each leaf a tale of sun and rain,
Of acorn dreams and playful gain.
With every flutter, giggles grow,
Nature's laughter, on the go.

The trees send greetings, winks abound,
In rustling whispers, joy is found.
These leafy postcards, oh so bright,
Bring sunshine, even in the night.

Bursting with Curiosity

A tiny nose, a twitchy tail,
Exploring life, with zest so frail.
With every step, new wonders greet,
A world of marvels, oh so sweet.

The twinkling eyes and endless glee,
Peeking behind each barked-up tree.
Turning over leaves, a treasure quest,
In the wild, our hearts are blessed.

Chasing shadows, dodging light,
Every moment feels so right.
With laughter bouncing all around,
In every nook, pure joy is found.

The Fluttering Pen

A little pen with wings of flair,
Darts around without a care.
It scribbles thoughts on leaves so green,
A whimsical wonder, rarely seen.

It writes of nuts and sunny days,
Of tripping toes in playful ways.
Every swoop, a giggling line,
An artist's world, simply divine.

The ink spills out like joyful streams,
Capturing life and all its dreams.
With every stroke, a chuckle found,
In every word, a silly sound.

A Jumble of Joy

In a basket filled with acorn cheer,
Are dreams and giggles, oh so dear.
A jumble here, a wiggle there,
Happiness rides upon the air.

With tiny paws, the treasures flop,
As laughter bubbles, never stop.
Rolling down with joyful noise,
In each small scrap, a world of joys.

The day unfolds in silly ways,
As fun and frolic fill the days.
A bundle bursting, smiles pour out,
In this chaos, there's no doubt.

A Whirl of Whimsy

Beneath the boughs, they dart and dash,
With tiny tails that swirl and flash.
Their cheeks, puffed up like fluffy clouds,
They chatter loud, drawing curious crowds.

Amid the leaves, they play and leap,
On branches high, they dare to creep.
A nut in hand, they scamper fast,
In this silly race, no time to last.

With acorns tossed and seeds displayed,
Their antics leave us all amazed.
In every nook, they seek a treat,
A wild little dance on furry feet.

So watch them twirl, those cheeky fellows,
In their own world, so bright and yellow.
Each twist and turn, a joyous spree,
Bringing smiles to you and me.

Kinetic Chronicles

In the park, they spin and twine,
Crafting chaos, oh so fine.
With acorns flying, laughter rings,
Each moment shared is fit for kings.

A leap, a bound, they shake the trees,
Very busy, doing as they please.
Chasing shadows, swift as air,
With hops and skips, they have no care.

Every twist brings a giggle near,
They play without a hint of fear.
They'll climb and dangle, give a wink,
In their silly fun, we all sink.

So let's rejoice in their mad dash,
Watching them twirl with a joyous splash.
For in this dance of fur and cheer,
Life's little moments are ever clear.

The Rustling Record

Whispers of fur in the gentle breeze,
Rustling leaves, they roam with ease.
Tiny paws upon the ground,
In every corner, joy is found.

A rustle here, a tumble there,
In every game, they have no care.
Through hoops of laughter, they make their way,
A rhythmic dance, brightening the day.

In a whirl of mischief, they conquer the climb,
Each tiny feat, a moment in time.
Pattering sounds lead us to glee,
A joyful chaos, such sights to see.

As they scribble tales through the leaves,
We laugh along, for joy never leaves.
In their wild world, we find respite,
In every rustle, pure delight.

Paws and Pages

With nimble paws, they turn the page,
In a storybook filled with sage.
Little plot twists come alive,
As they leap forth, a lively vibe.

Branches bend with every play,
Crafted antics in a funny way.
Each swish of tail, a chapter spun,
Where merriment and laughter run.

On leafy stages, they prance about,
In this playful plot, there's no doubt.
Pages flutter, hearts ignite,
In this furry tale, pure delight.

So join the dance, let laughter flow,
In their furry antics, joy will grow.
For every page they scurry through,
Brings a story warm and new.

Chatter from the Canopy

In the tree tops, giggles bloom,
Tiny tails make shadows loom.
Whispers echo, quick and sly,
A dance of leaves and a playful lie.

Nutty tales from acorn spheres,
Chattering loud, dismissing fears.
Branches sway with each small jest,
Nature's playground, a jolly fest.

Sunshine bursts through leafy ties,
Filled with laughter that never dies.
Paws at play, a vibrant spree,
Life's a game, as it should be!

Climbing high, they twist and twirl,
In a forest of fun, with a whirl.
Mischief lives in every leap,
Guard your snacks, or lose in heaps!

Playful Paws and Pencil Trails

Little creatures with nimble feet,
Dart around and skip the beat.
With tiny paws, they sketch and scroll,
Drawing chaos is their ultimate goal.

Crayons dropped on forest floor,
Artistry that never bore.
Rolling acorns, they create,
A masterpiece that swings the gate.

Crafty pranks as turns abound,
Chasing shadows, they zip around.
Whiskers twitch, and giggles burst,
In the wild, play is the first!

Under moonlight, they scamper free,
Chasing dreams with glistening glee.
Moments caught in a playful jive,
With every scribble, they come alive!

The Mischief of Mice on Mischief

In the meadow, whispers fly,
Tiny paws on a sneak and try.
Every nook holds a hidden prank,
Follow them to the joker's bank.

Cheese crumbs scattered like clues of fun,
Chasing giggles, on the run.
With bouncing tails and squeaky cheer,
Mischief thrives, it's perfectly clear.

Twist and turn, hide and seek,
With each rustle, the laughter peaks.
Round the bend, they scamper fast,
Creating moments that forever last.

In the night, when shadows dance,
They dip and dive, a merry prance.
Life's a riddle, a joyful tale,
With mice around, you will not fail!

Secrets Beneath the Oak

Underneath the grand oak tree,
Whispers of laughter, light and free.
Nutty secrets entwined in roots,
Where playful paws scour for loot.

Hidden treasures, acorns rare,
Magic carpets dance in the air.
With tiny giggles, they explore,
Life beneath the leafy floor.

In twilight glows, they share a snack,
Nibbling softly, then bounce back.
Tales of mischief, a nightly game,
Each one burst with a spark of fame.

What's more fun than a secret spree?
Hiding treasures, just wait and see!
Under the oak, where joy is sown,
A world of wonders is brightly grown!

Scribbled Secrets Above the Ground

In trees so high, secrets bloom,
Nuts tucked away in a leafy room.
Paws scratch the bark with great delight,
Sharing whispers in the soft twilight.

A chubby friend with a twitchy tail,
Chasing dreams along the trail.
Leaves giggle as they swish and sway,
Architects of mischief at play.

He gathers treasures, so shiny and bright,
Hiding them well, out of plain sight.
With every leap and daring bound,
Giggles echo, a joyful sound.

The forest smiles, a merry place,
Nature tickles with its playful grace.
In every nook, a tale unfolds,
Of silly antics and treasures told.

A Dance of Shadows and Sunshine

Beneath the sun, on a leafy stage,
Tiny feet prance, full of rage.
A swirl of tails and a flash of fur,
Nature's ballet, a delightful stir.

Branches sway to a whimsical beat,
As frolicsome paws hop on their feet.
The sunlight winks through the canopy,
While giggling echoes from the leafy sea.

A pirouette here, a comic roll there,
Shadows blend with the bright, warm air.
With every leap, laughter ignites,
As woodland critters dance through the nights.

Chasing each other, darting with glee,
The world feels light, wild, and free.
Every stumble, a chuckle or two,
In this lively realm, where fun's never blue.

Woodland Whispers

In the thicket where the giggles grow,
Woodland creatures put on a show.
Chatter and clamor fill the air,
With secrets shared, without a care.

Leaves rustle softly, conspiracies bloom,
In hidden nooks, laughter finds room.
Nuts as currency in a trade of delight,
Whimsical meetings in the glow of twilight.

Little critters dance on the ground,
Chasing each other, round and round.
With twitchy noses and beady eyes,
They spark the joy that never dies.

Under the stars, mischief unfolds,
Every whisper a tale, every giggle bold.
In a world of chatter, so quirky and bright,
Woodland creatures bask in moonlight.

The Acorn Chronicle

Once upon a time in the forest green,
Acorns gathered, all shiny and keen.
Tiny hands clutch them, stashing away,
For a winter feast on a cold, gray day.

Stories told of the great acorn race,
Where nimble paws found their own pace.
With leaps and bounds, they scurried in glee,
A forest full of wild jubilee.

At dusk, the moon shared a glowing grin,
As laughter echoed where the fun begins.
Gathering friends for a nibble and cheer,
Every acorn a treasure, held dear.

From tiny tales of fluff and delight,
To bold adventures in the night.
The chronicles spin, as time spins round,
In every kernel, joy is found.

Rambunctious Romp

In the park, they dart and dash,
Fluffy tails in a wild splash.
Chasing leaves that twirl and glide,
Under trees, they shriek with pride.

Nuts are hidden, treasures found,
With little leaps, they scurry 'round.
Giggles echo through the air,
As they plot mischief with a flair.

A clumsy slip, a tumble down,
With fluffed-up tails, they bounce around.
Each little giggle, every squeal,
Makes the day's fun truly real.

When day is done, as shadows creep,
They curl up close, exhausted sleep.
Dreaming of the next big chase,
In their minds, an endless race.

Mischievous Memories

On a branch, they peek and spy,
Stealing seeds as time flies by.
With tiny paws and crafty ways,
Creating chaos in bright sun rays.

Acorns tossed like little bombs,
Making messes, oh how it calms!
A haphazard dance, a furry spree,
Tickles of laughter, wild and free.

In the garden, seeds they sow,
A tiny storm with quite the show.
Each little nibble, each big thrill,
Reminds us joy is such a skill.

When evening falls, they scamper home,
With tales of fun in their little dome.
Memories stitched in playful flight,
Under starry skies, good night, good night!

Raindrop Ruminations

Pitter-patter on the ground,
Little paws make a joyful sound.
Splashing puddles, oh what fun!
Chasing raindrops in the sun.

With every drip, a silly dance,
Furry feet take every chance.
Laughter echoes with each leap,
As they play, their joy runs deep.

Swirling whirlwinds, a splashy blast,
In muddy tracks, their fun is cast.
Painting paths in rainy weather,
Frolicking together, light as a feather.

When the clouds begin to part,
With tired tails and happy heart,
They find a nook, all snug and dry,
Dreaming of the next swoopy sky.

Paws on Paper

Oh, what mischief starts to brew,
When tiny paws create anew.
Dancing on a page so white,
With scribbles, oh what a sight!

Inky trails with giggles loud,
Artful chaos, we are proud!
A masterpiece of wild delight,
Every stroke a joyful bite.

Crayon colors, a joyful mix,
Pawprints left in wiggly flicks.
Each creation tells a tale,
Of furry artists who prevail.

When the papers start to stack,
With giggles loud, we can't hold back.
A gallery of silly cheer,
Memories made, we hold them dear.

Mischief on the Move

With fluffy tails and tiny paws,
They scamper quick, not a moment to pause.
Chasing shadows, they leap and bound,
In a leafy playground where fun's abound.

Nutty treasures tucked away tight,
They plot mischief from dawn till night.
A sneaky peek, a daring dash,
With giggles echoing, they dash and clash.

Doodles of Delight

Sketching circles 'round the park,
Drawing giggles from all they embark.
With a nibble here and a nibble there,
Their silly antics fill the air.

Crisscrossing pathways, they leave a trace,
A whimsical dance, a playful race.
Leaves become canvases, bright and bold,
Their artistic flair, a sight to behold.

Acorns and Adventures

Acorns scattered, a treasure trove,
Each nut a tale of the mischief they wove.
Racing through the tall green grass,
They chase the wind, let worries pass.

Jumping high with a gleeful shout,
Launching acorns, spinning about.
In the heart of the woods, laughter rings,
As tiny explorers discover what spring brings.

Scamps in the Sunlight

Basking in beams, they take a seat,
Nibbling snacks, oh what a treat!
With wriggles and twists, they spark delight,
Chasing sunbeams in pure daylight.

Flipping leaves, they play a game,
Every day different, never the same.
Under the branches where shadows play,
Life is a circus, hip-hip-hooray!

Leaves and Leaps

In the trees, they flit and dart,
Chasing shadows, a vibrant art.
With a flick and a fluff, they rise,
Racing 'gainst the autumn skies.

Each leaf a stage, each twig a prop,
In their world, the fun won't stop.
They tumble down from bough to ground,
With cheeky glee, they spin around.

A dance of joy on branches wide,
Nature's jesters, they do not hide.
With acorn caps as their fine hats,
Playing games with giggling spats.

When the sun dips low, the fun persists,
In the dusk, adventure twists.
Under the moon, they leap and play,
Till sleepiness drives them away.

Woodland Whispers

In the hush of the wooded scene,
Tiny chatter fills the green.
With fluffy cheeks and tiny feet,
Their secret meetings are quite the treat.

Chasing tales of nuts and seeds,
They plot and scheme with joyful leads.
Each moment shared, a spark of mirth,
Their laughter echoes through the earth.

With winks and nods, they swap their snacks,
Grand stories told of daring hacks.
Life in the branches, a playful sport,
With every rustle, a joyful report.

As twilight falls, the whispers fade,
Yet in their hearts, the joy won't trade.
With a final leap, they scurry and race,
Leaving behind a giggling trace.

Tales of a Tail-Twirler

There once was a twirler, tail a swirl,
In a circus of leaves, she had a whirl.
With acorn tricks and flips so rad,
Every leap made the woodland glad.

Her friends would gather, eyes aglow,
Each daring stunt, a thrilling show.
They'd laugh and cheer with every twist,
In the forest, none could resist.

With a whoop, she dove from a limb,
Her acrobatic flair, never dim.
In the spotlight of sunbeams bright,
She danced through the air, a pure delight.

As dusk set in, they'd climb back high,
Under the stars, their spirits fly.
No tale was complete without her spin,
The brightest star in their woodland din.

Nutty Notebooks

In a cozy nook, the critters write,
Of all the fun from day to night.
With tiny paws, they scrawl and scratch,
Every acorn tale, a perfect match.

From nutty heists to daring leaps,
The pages fill with giggling peeps.
Chronicles of crunch, during their feast,\nEach line penned, a joyful beast.

In each little book, a world unfolds,
Of wild adventures and tales retold.
With illustrations, they make a scene,
The funniest moments in all that's seen.

At the end of the day, they pass their finds,
Sharing laughter with open minds.
In the fields of gold where memories weave,
Nutty notebooks, forever they leave.

Whiskers' Wandering Words

In a world of nuts and cheer,
Tails twitching, never fear,
Chasing shadows, oh so spry,
They leap and laugh, oh my, oh my!

With acorns piled in a ball,
Pouncing hard, they never fall,
Snickers echo through the trees,
Whispers dancing on the breeze.

Charming chatter fills the air,
With little leaps and charming flair,
Tiny feet that scurry fast,
Creating giggles, unsurpassed.

A wiggly dance, a cheeky show,
In the park, they steal the glow,
With jests and jives, they rule the day,
In their frolic, joy's on display.

Gentle Jumps in the Glow

Beneath the sun, they bound and play,
Fluffy dreams in golden rays,
Twitching noses, brightened eyes,
A comedy of leaps and sighs.

With chubby cheeks, they grab and munch,
In a whirlwind of a playful bunch,
Tumbles turn into silly falls,
Giggles echo, through the halls.

Funny capers, all around,
Nuts and tricks are truly found,
As they wiggle on the ground,
Joyful antics, laughter's sound.

In twilight's blush, they dance with glee,
A vibrant cast of folly-free,
With every hop, a cheerful tune,
Their gentle jumps beneath the moon.

Scribbles in the Sunlight

In sunlit parks where shadows fade,
With fluffy tails, they parade,
Cracking jokes with every split,
As they scamper and they'll flit.

Paws at play on grassy dreams,
With every dash, the laughter beams,
Twists and turns in playful style,
Every wiggle brings a smile.

Chasing leaves like little whirls,
Through the air, the laughter curls,
With a wink and a fluffy cheer,
They scribble joy from ear to ear.

In splashes bright of golden light,
Their lively jests steal every sight,
With acorn hats, they strut with pride,
In this funny world, they'll glide.

Forest Folios

Within the woods, they scribe their tales,
In funny lines amidst the trails,
With hops and skips and cheerful sounds,
The storytelling joy abounds.

Chubby cheeks with acorn pens,
They write their mischief, never ends,
Pages flutter, breezy fun,
Crafting riddles 'til the day is done.

In leafy nooks where laughter springs,
They weave their notes with tiny strings,
Each forest folio a giddy plan,
By tiny paws of nature's band.

Through whispered leaves, their secrets flow,
In every giggle, a great show,
With sketches wild in nature's book,
They share the fun in every nook.

Flurries of Fur

In the garden, a dash of brown,
Tiny paws race up and down.
Nuts in tow, they scurry and play,
Bouncing around in a furry ballet.

With a flick of their tails so spry,
They leap with laughter, oh my, oh my!
Chasing their shadows under the sun,
These little furballs are always on the run.

When they wiggle, it's quite a sight,
Chomping acorns with all their might.
In a whirlwind, they make their home,
Flurries of fur, they freely roam.

As the leaves twist and twirl in the breeze,
These charming creatures are sure to please.
With a hop, skip, and a mischievous wink,
In the world of antics, they're the missing link.

Autumn's Agile Acrobat

Through branches high, they dart and weave,
Acrobats in autumn, who could believe?
With a flip and a twist, they defy the ground,
Their antics echo a playful sound.

A parade of fluff, with eyes so bright,
They pirouette under the soft twilight.
Creating a ruckus, they leap and swing,
In the theater of trees, they rule as kings.

Falling leaves like confetti around,
They dance through the air, barely making a sound.
With a nuts-filled pouch, they plot and scheme,
Bringing laughter to nature, like a wild dream.

As twilight falls, their fun won't cease,
In a world of hilarity, they find their peace.
These agile acrobats, bold and spry,
Turn autumn days into a comedy sky.

Tiny Tails in Twilight

As the sun dips low and shadows grow,
These tiny tails dart to and fro.
With a twitch of whiskers, a giggle erupts,
In the golden light, their silliness jumps.

Chasing each other in a surrounding glow,
Their goofy glances make mischief flow.
They tumble and tumble, in graceful glee,
These playful nights are a sight to see.

In the hushed whispers of evening's embrace,
They scamper and scamper, a wild chase.
Silly squeaks and laughter keep time,
As tiny tails twirl in nature's rhyme.

When stars blanket the sky so clear,
These merry little creatures bring joy and cheer.
In twinkling twilight, their fun won't fail,
With tiny tails dancing, they'll always prevail.

Chaotic Chatter

In the forest, you'll hear a sound,
A cacophony of chatter all around.
With nutty banter and playful squeaks,
These lively ones bring joy for weeks.

Jumping to and fro, they share the news,
Their chaotic gossip, a quirky muse.
From high in the branches, they shout with glee,
In their whimsical world, they wish to be free.

Nuts get tossed in a playful duel,
Smart little critters, they're nobody's fool.
With bursts of laughter, they share delight,
Their humor fills the air, morning and night.

So grab some popcorn, sit right down,
And join the fun with this furry clown.
In a whirlwind of chatter and whirlwinds spins,
These little jokers bring joy with their grins.

Tales from the Twisted Branch

On a branch high above, they prance with cheer,
Chasing their shadows, with nothing to fear.
With a flick of a tail, they zoom to the sky,
Feathers all ruffled when they zoom right by.

With acorns galore, they stash and they stash,
Tunneling treasures, oh, what a bash!
Furry little bandits, full of delight,
Stashing their seeds, both day and night.

One little fellow, a master of style,
In his nutty little coat, he winks with a smile.
He held a grand council among all his friends,
"More nuts for winter? The fun never ends!"

So if you look up, a flick and a dash,
You might just catch them, all set for a splash.
With laughter and giggles, they pirouette around,
In tales from the branches, pure joy can be found.

Sketches of a Scurrying Soul

In the morning sunlight, they dance and they leap,
Chasing their dreams where acorn piles heap.
With spirals of joy, they scribble on air,
Crafting their journeys without a care.

A canvas of leaves and a sketch of the trees,
Each twist and each turn, a whimsical breeze.
With laughter that echoes through the bright foliage,
They leave little footprints, a furry collage.

One jumps with delight, a tumble and roll,
While making wild art with nature's own scroll.
Each caper a stroke on the canvas so green,
In this wild gallery, what a sight to be seen!

So if you stand still, let your giggles unfold,
Watch the masters create, both brave and bold.
Their charming antics, a playful parade,
In sketches of life, memories are made.

The Art of Trees and Tails

In the whispering woods, where mischief unfolds,
Tiny acrobats flip, with stories untold.
Each leap a brushstroke, each dash a new tale,
Painting the sky with their whirlwinds of sail.

With tails like paintbrushes, they color the air,
Crafting wild art with giggles to spare.
Each branch a new start, each leaf a decree,
"Let's hop and let's spin, just you and me!"

As they scurry and scamper, a symphony plays,
Cheerful mischief filling sunlit bays.
They gather their laughter, like treasures to keep,
In the art of the trees, where the wild ones leap.

So come join the fun, take a peek and behold,
The art of the tails, both daring and bold.
With each hearty chuckle, life dances with glee,
In the gallery of twigs, there's magic to see.

Hidden Treasures among the Leaves

Beneath the tall trees, where the sunlight doth weave,
Little ones scatter, with treasures to leave.
Nuts here and there, a playful delight,
In the whispers of leaves, they scamper from sight.

With cheeks full of goodies, they giggle and tease,
Creating a ruckus, oh, what a breeze!
The dance of the leafy, a playful ballet,
As treasures of nature come out to play.

"Finders are keepers!" the small critters cheer,
In their treasure-filled pantry, they hold it so dear.
Each hidden delight, a prize to uphold,
From the earth to the branches, in stories retold.

So wander the woods, take a moment, just pause,
Join in their laughter, embrace their wild cause.
In hidden adventures, let joys interweave,
You'll find funny treasures, right there among leaves.

Dreams of the Bushy Bandit

In the treetops high, he dreams away,
With acorns as jewels, he plans his play.
A bandit of fluff, with a tail held proud,
He chats with the clouds, sings loud to the crowd.

With eyes like tiny marbles, bright and keen,
He scampers and dances, a woodland machine.
Plotting his heists in the moon's gentle glow,
Stealing hearts more than nuts, as he puts on a show.

Each branch is a stage for this little thief,
His tales of mischief bring laughter and relief.
From dawn until dusk, he's a bundle of cheer,
The bushy-tailed rogue, spreading joy far and near.

His dreams have no limits, they twist and they twine,
In the world of the green, he makes every vine.
With humor so rich and antics so grand,
The bushy bandit's a true woodland brand.

Curiosity and Climbing

With a twitch of his nose and a leap in the air,
He climbs up the branches, without a care.
Curiosity calls with a flick of his tail,
Exploring the secrets in every detail.

He peeks in the nests where the birds tell their tales,
And chases the shadows as daylight pales.
Nothing's too high for his nimble ascent,
Every bend of the bark is a new testament.

Atop of the world, he surveys his land,
A realm of adventure at his small hands.
The forest a puzzle, with mysteries bright,
With nuts as the treasures, discoveries in sight.

With laughter in leaps and a dash in his play,
He conquers the trees in a magical way.
Curiosity drives him, what else could it be?
He giggles with glee, oh so wild and free!

The Nimble Notetaker

A tiny notetaker with fur so divine,
Jots down his findings with acorn and twine.
With measured precision, he scribbles and scrawls,
Recording the antics of critters and brawls.

He jots down the tales as he darts to and fro,
Of rabbits at lunch and the badger's grand show.
His notebook filled with the odd and the fun,
With doodles and sketches of frolic and run.

In every swift movement, a story unfolds,
Of friendships and games, of brave hearts so bold.
The nimble notetaker, with humor so near,
Captures the laughter of all who draw near.

Every scribble a window to woodland delight,
As he fills up his pages in morning's soft light.
With each little note, he captures the cheer,
The forest's own laughter, forever held dear.

Whims of the Whiskers

With whiskers a-dancing, he stirs up some fun,
Chasing after shadows and rays of the sun.
The whims of his whiskers lead him on a spree,
A playful mischief-maker, wild and carefree.

Through leaves that are rustling, he prances around,
A bundle of laughter with joy that knows no bound.
He high-fives the branches, does flips with a grin,
While gathering giggles and nuts tucked within.

His tail's a wild banner of joy in the breeze,
Spinning and swirling with effortless ease.
Whims of the whiskers, he brings forth the glee,
A creature of chaos, as funny as can be.

As day turns to dusk, he settles to rest,
In dreams filled with antics, he thinks he's the best.
With a giggle and squeak, he slips deep into night,
For tomorrow he'll play with his heart full of light.

Sunlit Scribbles

In the golden sun, they dart and play,
Chasing tails in a lively array.
Nutty notes fill the air with glee,
As they leap from branch to blossoming tree.

Their tiny hands clutch acorn dreams,
With hops and skips, they weave bright schemes.
Chirps and chuckles echo in delight,
As shadows dance beneath the light.

With fuzzy leaps from heights so grand,
They scribble joy across the land.
Each jump a stroke in nature's art,
Furry artists with a merry heart.

Amidst the leaves, their laughter grows,
In every twist, mischief flows.
Sunlit scribbles of joy unbound,
In playful chaos, life is found.

The Dance of the Tree-Dweller

Bouncing around, the fun begins,
With each acrobatic twist, they grin.
Nuts and giggles fly through the breeze,
The tree-dweller dances with flair and ease.

Whirling through branches, a comical sight,
Fluffy tailed dancers, bounding in flight.
With a leap and a flip, they sway with joy,
Each move a frolic, no care to annoy.

Flipping and swirling, they prance so spry,
Tickling the leaves as they pass by.
In circles and spirals, they twirl about,
Creating a whirl of laughter and shouts.

Beneath the canopy, they steal the show,
With a nutty performance, antics in tow.
The dance of the tree-dweller is a true delight,
A merry parade from morning till night.

Woodland Wonderment

In the heart of the woods, where laughter reigns,
Furry little sprites unleash their refrains.
With dashes and dives, they explore the trees,
In Woodland wonder, they dance with the breeze.

Around the old oaks, they zoom and twirl,
Creating a ruckus, watch their tails whirl.
Chasing shadows, they leap and bound,
In this woodland playground, joy can be found.

With friends by their side, they scurry and play,
Each nut a treasure, brightening the day.
In wonderment's grip, they frolic and tease,
Scribbling memories in soft rustling leaves.

Every nook and cranny hides a surprise,
With laughter and mischief under the skies.
In the magical woods, where spirits convene,
Life's little wonders are evergreen.

Scribbles Among the Pines

Amidst the pines, a lively spree,
Chubby bodies bouncing, wild and free.
Scribbles of mischief paint the air,
As the little ones tumble without a care.

With their beady eyes and twitching tails,
They bounce and chatter, leaving trails.
In a flurry of fluff and playful quips,
Every step giggles, every jump flips.

Leaping from bough to bough with glee,
Crafting their stories up high in the tree.
Amidst the needles, laughter rings clear,
Scribbles of joy that we hold dear.

As dusk approaches, they snuggle tight,
Huddled together, resting in sight.
Among the pines, where fun never ends,
Their scribbles echo, our furry little friends.

Forest Fables Untold

In the woods where nutty dreams reside,
Tiny paws journey, no need to hide.
Chasing tails with a flick and a spin,
Every tool in the toolbox, ready to win.

Leaves rustle like whispers, secrets in air,
Acorns roll down, a bouncing affair.
Jumps and tumbles, they frolic about,
In this leafy realm, there's never a doubt.

A dance on the branches, a leap through the sun,
Their giggles echo, oh what silly fun!
With bushy-tailed flair, they twirl and they hop,
Making mischief, they'll never stop!

Underneath the great sky, they all play their part,
Tales made of twirls, straight from the heart.
In this merry playground, laughter does swell,
Forest fables untold, they weave and they tell.

Acorn Adventures

Marketing nuts with a swagger so grand,
Tiny adventurers, all part of the band.
A map drawn in soil, their treasure to find,
Unraveling secrets that nature designed.

Up in a tree, they plot with delight,
Imagining travels by day and by night.
Oh, the acorn snacks and the games they will play,
Fetching delights while the shadows sway.

"Let's race to the brook!" one enthusiast cried,
With flurry and speed, their laughter the guide.
But one little fella tripped on a root,
Rolling down gently, all curled like a fruit!

They giggled and chuckled, no tears in their eyes,
For adventure is sweeter with laughter that flies.
All the antics, the tales that they weave,
In acorn adventures, it's fun to believe!

Fluttering Fur and Fancy

Up in the treetops where the breezes dance,
Furry creatures prance in a blissful chance.
With hearts full of mischief and eyes all aglow,
They twirl and they whirl, putting on a show.

Fancy little hats, a pinecone for flair,
With whispers of magic floating through the air.
They dress in the leaves, a colorful sight,
Creating a carnival, pure delight.

One twirls on a branch, the other takes flight,
Giggles and squeaks fill the warm summer night.
Fluffy tails twinkle, like stars in a dream,
It's pandemonium wrapped in a beam!

With each little game, joy darker than night,
Fluttering fur takes off in delight.
In this raucous theater where spirits are free,
Fancy is the tune, and laughter's the key.

Writings in the Bark

In the whisper of woods, stories abound,
Tales etched in bark where secrets are found.
With tiny little paws, they scribble with glee,
Telling the tales of all they can see.

The mischief of midnight, the ruckus of day,
They jot down the laughter, the games, and the play.
A doodle of acorns, a sketch of a chase,
Writings in bark, bring smiles to each face.

"Look here!" cries the one, "I've drawn your great leap!"
"I've captured your tumble, your secrets to keep!"
They gather around, their eyes shining bright,
Sharing their stories 'til the fall of night.

So in the rough wood, with each twist and turn,
These moments of joy eternally burn.
In the heart of the forest, so wild and so stark,
Legends are written, with joy in each mark.

Hopping through Horizons

Paws prance lightly on the ground,
A nutty treasure to be found.
With twitching tail and joyous leaps,
A dance of laughter, the forest keeps.

Branches shake with giggles bright,
Chasing tails in the warm sunlight.
Fluffy hats and tiny feet,
Nature's jesters, oh what a treat!

Mischief woven in every twist,
In shady nooks, none can resist.
The world spins round with each small hop,
A circus act that'll never stop.

Clever stunts that take the eye,
While sneaky snacks just fly on by.
With every dash and playful fun,
A tale unfolds, we've just begun.

Nature's Notepad

In the leafy realm where mischief swirls,
Tiny paws bring joy unfurl.
With acorns tucked in cozy beds,
They scribble tales with wiggly threads.

A canvas bright of flickering leaves,
Where every twist brings giggly heaves.
With twirls and dips, they paint the air,
Nature's canvas, a merry affair.

Knotty branches, a slippery slide,
Jumps and giggles they graciously ride.
Each crinkled nut, a story to share,
Filled with laughter floating everywhere.

Under the sun, feelings soar,
Each giggle bounces, forever more.
Life's a joke on this spinning wheel,
In the book of life, they write and feel.

Scribbling Shadows

Shadows flit through the sunlit trees,
Chasing dreams on a playful breeze.
With fuzzy tails and cheeky grins,
   A comic strip of furry wins.

Nimbly darting in shadows they creep,
Across the park where secrets sleep.
With every leap, the world they sketch,
   Giggles erupt, and joy is etched.

Bouncing over logs, a zany crew,
With disappearing acts, they bid adieu.
Each scratch and rustle brings forth glee,
Writing tales of whimsy, wild and free.

In the twilight, their laughter fades,
Whispering antics as daylight wades.
From silly dances to playful flights,
The echoes linger through starry nights.

The Elusive Quill

Tiny paws with a pen in hand,
Sketching joy across the land.
Each little nib, a world to yield,
A masterwork in the open field.

Wiggly lines and dots of cheer,
Funny doodles that draw near.
With each scurry, tales emerge,
In nature's book, ideas surge.

With curious hops, they craft their art,
Creating laughter, a joyful heart.
An elusive quill, a tiny muse,
In every hop, new paths they choose.

Under the moon, their secrets dwell,
Banters and giggles, a hilarious spell.
A whimsical dance among the trees,
As stories flutter, carried by breeze.

Flicks of Furry Folly

In the branches high they dart,
With a flurry, a little heart.
Chasing tails in loops and swirls,
Spreading joy in tiny twirls.

Nutty treasures on the ground,
With a chatter, they abound.
In the breeze, their laughter flies,
Clever moves and clever lies.

Woodland pals join the show,
With a bounce and a playful throw.
Every leap is a new trick,
Each mischief, a little flick.

As the sun begins to fade,
They gather 'round for the parade.
With a giggle and a cheer,
Furry folly, all are near.

Mischief in the Meadow

In the grass, a scamper bright,
Tiny feet take off in flight.
With a hop, a skip, a dash,
They dart in every zippy flash.

Whiskers twitching, eyes aglow,
Creating chaos, putting on a show.
With each leap, a giggly squeal,
Mischief planned and oh so real!

Gathering acorns, a playful race,
Tossing seeds in every space.
Running wild, the laughter flows,
Their cheeky dance, no one knows.

As the moon peeks from the trees,
They settle down with gentle ease.
With dreams of pranks yet to scheme,
In the meadow, all's a dream.

Sprightly Shadows

Beneath the sky, bright as can be,
They dash and dart so carelessly.
Shadows flicker, tails on high,
Sprightly leaps that touch the sky.

In the glade, a twirl and spin,
Watch them whirl, let the fun begin.
With a playful nudge and a tease,
They dance around with such sweet ease.

Branches bend with every bound,
Whispered secrets all around.
With every twist, they take a turn,
Chasing shadows as they learn.

The evening falls, a quiet hush,
Still as statues, a comic rush.
In playful dreams, they bounce and roam,
Sprightly shadows call them home.

The Jumping Jotter

A little scribble in the air,
With splashes of color everywhere.
Pencils poised on tiny toes,
What they write, nobody knows!

Pages flip with a joyful spree,
Each tiny scribble, wild and free.
With a hop, a jolt, a laugh,
Crafting tales on their behalf.

In the park, they leap and glide,
With every jump, they feel the pride.
Jotting down the day's delight,
Each little moment, pure and bright.

As the stars begin to peek,
With a flip, their laughter's chic.
Jotters jump from here to there,
In the night, just like a dare.

www.ingramcontent.com/pod-product-compliance
Lightning Source LLC
Chambersburg PA
CBHW051640160426
43209CB00004B/725